Services Framework Implementation Guide

Services Framework – Implementation Guide

Implementation of the Solution

David Bright & Paul Freeman

Disclaimer

The content provided herein is for educational purposes and does not take the place of professional legal or business advice consultation. Every effort has been made to ensure that the content provided in this guide is accurate and helpful for our readers at publishing time. However, this is not an exhaustive treatment of the subjects. No liability is assumed for losses or damages due to the information provided. You are responsible for your own choices, actions, and results. You should consult your attorney for your specific publishing and disclaimer questions and needs.

Copyright

Services Framework – Implementation Guide by David Bright and Paul Freeman. Published by Professional Development Partners, Inc. 470 Merida Drive, Santa Barbara, CA 93111

www.prodevpartners.com

© 2019 Professional Development Partners, Inc.

All rights reserved. No portion of this book may be reproduced in any form without permission from the publisher, except as permitted by U.S. copyright law. For permissions contact:

pfreeman@prodevpartners.com

ISBN: 978-1-09558-171-1

Table of Contents

Disclaimer iv
Copyright iv
Preface vii
   Services Framework – Implementation Guide vii
About This Guide viii
   Guide Overview viii
   Intended Audience viii
   Why Is This Important? viii
Overview ix
    Prerequisites x
Chapter 1: Project Planning 1
   Required Documentation 1
     System Design 2
     Feature and Function Design (optional, depending on the solution) 2
     Physical Design 2
     Device-level Design 2
     Operations Design 2
   Project Management Plan 2
   Escalation Plan 3
   Communications Plan 4
   Project Kick-Off Meetings 4
   Key Steps for Project Planning 5
   Action Plan 5
Chapter 2. Solution Staging 7
   Key Steps for Staging 7
   Action Plan 8
Chapter 3. Phased implementation 9
    Solution Implementation 10

    Pilot Implementation and Testing 11
    Device Implementation 11
    Key Steps for Phased Implementation 12
    Action Plan 13

Chapter 4. Full System Migration 15
    Full System Migration Process 15
    Key Steps for System Migration 16
    Action Plan 17

Chapter 5. Acceptance Testing 19
    Key Steps for Acceptance Testing 19
    Action Plan 20

Chapter 6. Staff Training 21
    End User Training 21
    Key Steps for End User Training 21
    Action Plan 22
    Administrator and Help Desk Training 23
    Key Steps for Administrator and Help Desk Training 23
    Action Plan 24

Chapter 7. Post Implementation Support 25
    Key Steps for Post Implementation Support 25
    Action Plan 26

Chapter 8. Operations Implementation 27
    Key Steps for Operations Implementation 27
    Action Plan 28

Chapter 9. Project Closeout 29
    Key Steps for Project Closeout 30
    Action Plan 30

Chapter 10: How to Measure Your Success 33

Preface

Over the past few decades, we have developed a collection of guides to help IT solution provider companies provide repeatable, successful, and profitable customer engagements.

These guides are designed to assist IT solution provider companies in improving their service practice capabilities and to reinforce their current investments in people, process, and tools with best-in-class methodologies and approaches.

The guides provide solution provider employees, owners and managers with a "how to" approach together with essential information to determine what to implement, including executable action plans, tools, and templates.

Services Framework – Implementation Guide

This guide is focused on the implement phase of the typical IT Services Lifecycle as depicted in the following diagram.

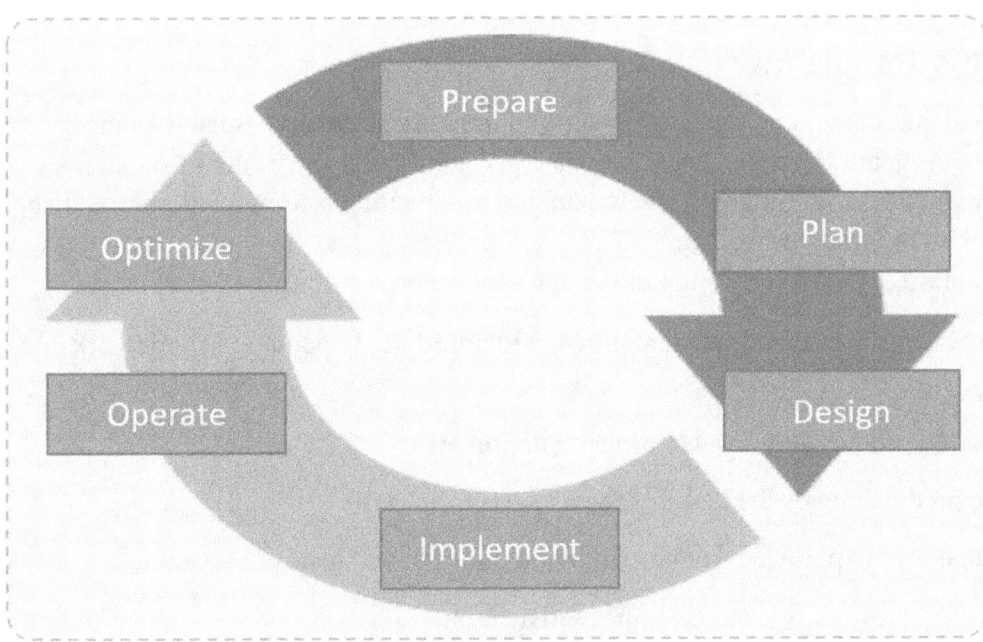

About This Guide

Guide Overview

This guide provides information for IT solution provider companies around building a solution implementation framework. Following the approaches and best practices described in this guide will help your organization effectively and consistently install, configure, migrate, stage, and make operational customer solutions.

Intended Audience

This guide is intended for new project and program managers, and for experienced project managers with expertise in other fields, who are transitioning into PM roles in IT Solution Provider companies.

In IT solution provider companies, project managers operating in the following departments will find this guide useful:

- Project Management
- Delivery Engineering

Why Is This Important?

A well-defined, structured approach to IT solution implementation will enable your technical delivery team to implement solutions consistently and according to standards, thereby reducing the time-to-deliver and enhancing the overall customer experience. The solutions will incorporate technical and organizational best practices, while continuing to build on the intellectual property and knowledge of your organization.

Some of the benefits associated with creating a structured implementation framework include:

- Increased productivity for the implementation team.
- More predictable results through consistent execution.
- A transfer of experience from the individual into the company.
- Increased profitability and customer satisfaction.

What are the measurable key performance indicators or skills required?

- Structured implementation framework defined and in place.
- Knowledge management system and processes.

- Hardware implementation skills, procedures, and best practices.
- Legacy system integration skills and procedures.
- Device deployment skills and processes.
- System migration skills and processes.
- Customer staff training content, skills, and processes.
- Implementation support skills and processes.
- System acceptance testing skills and processes.
- Operations implementation skills and processes.
- Project closure templates, formats, and processes.

Overview

The implementation framework includes activities that you conduct during the final deployment phase of a typical IT engagement. While it is possible for you to sell the implementation phase as a standalone service, it is more commonly part of an end-to-end solution that is preceded by several other phases. Together, these phases make up the Services Lifecycle.

Implementing an IT system or solution for a customer can be a complex exercise and will require a substantial amount of knowledge and expertise on the part of your technical delivery team.

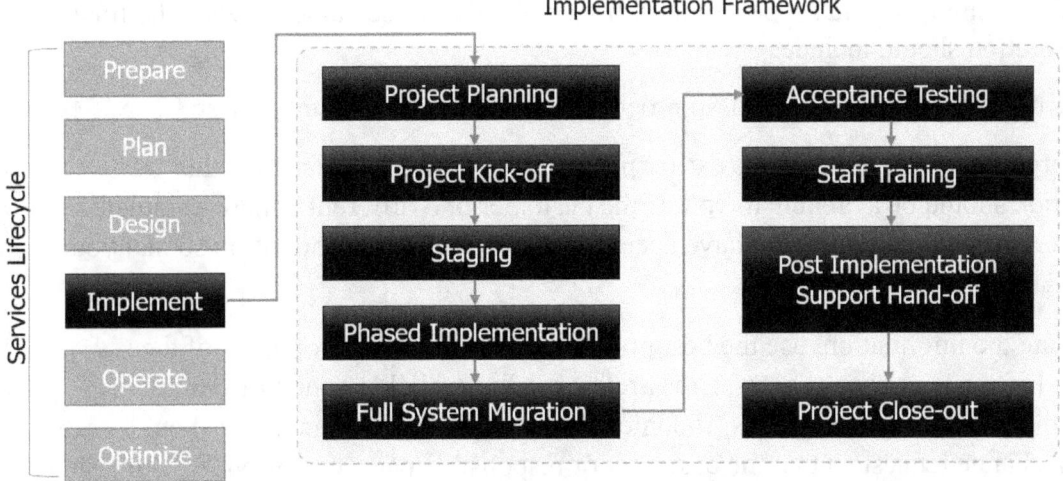

Figure 1. Implementation Framework

The implementation framework relies on the deliverables from the earlier Prepare, Plan and Design phases of the Services Lifecycle. The key activities in the implementation phase use the overall project management plan and design deliverables. Primarily, the implementation phase turns the design and plans into reality through the application of standard project management methodologies and processes.

As indicated in the figure above, the Implementation Phase includes several sub-elements that make up the implementation framework. You must complete each sub-element for each engagement to fully deploy a solution that meets the customer requirements and has the prescribed features and functionality.

Each implementation framework sub-element is described in more detail in this document.

In addition to the implementation framework, your organization should establish and maintain a repository of technical delivery content that is mapped to the services your organization delivers to customers. You will use this content when you create each element in the implementation framework, and it will form the basis of your knowledge management system.

Prerequisites

Before starting the implementation phase, it is important to have the following:

- Background information from the Prepare, Plan, and Design phases.
- Design and planning information from the design phase.
- Solution vision and scope details, which will aid in understanding what the final solution should include.
- Customer's design approval to proceed with the implementation phase.

If your organization completed the earlier phases of the Services Lifecycle, this information should be available to you. If the customer or a different vendor completed the earlier phases, make sure you have access to all the required information so that you can validate it.

To validate the information, use the best practice guides from earlier phases of the Services Lifecycle as check sheets. Cross-reference the available content to each deliverable defined in those guides. If content is incomplete or missing, you should initiate a change request so that the customer or responsible party can provide the missing information.

The account manager from your organization, who is responsible for the customer relationship, should build a contingency into the statement of work for this phase to cover any additional costs that your organization may be incurred to compile the missing information.

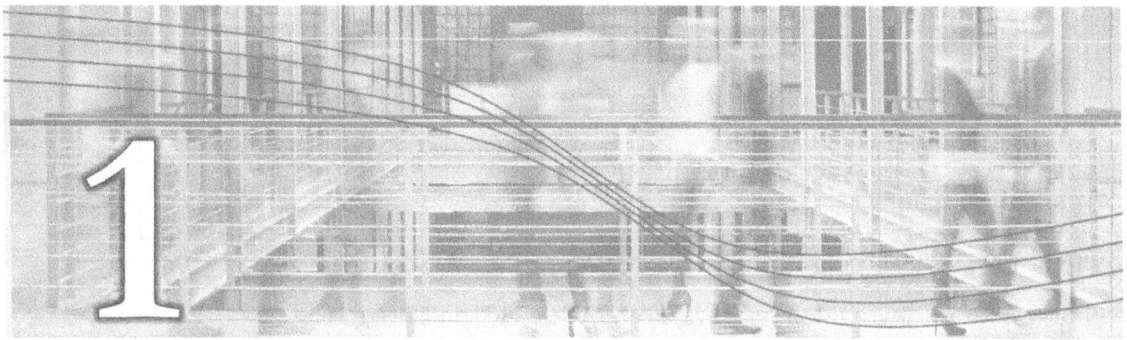

Chapter 1: Project Planning

Required Documentation

The Prepare, Plan, and Design phases in the Services Lifecycle lead to the Implementation phase. You will use all the deliverables from these prior steps to implement a successful solution.

There is a difference, however, between a high-level system design document and the detailed instructions and information required to implement and deploy a complex solution. For this reason, prior to the start of the implementation phase, be sure your team has access to all the required documentation and content at the appropriate level of detail. This is referred to as delivery-ready content.

The required content includes all necessary background information, such as:

- The business case for the solution.
- The vision and scope for the solution.
- Details about the existing infrastructure and systems.

The implementation team needs this information to understand the environment and any special requirements or constraints, and to be able to implement the solution accordingly.

If the customer awarded the end-to-end solution to your organization, your implementation team should have access to all this information in the right format and the correct level of detail. If any part of the content is lacking, call upon the responsible party to remedy the situation. If this is not possible, you should initiate a change request to build into the project the additional time, resource, and cost requirements for gathering the additional content.

The required content typically includes deliverables, data, and information from the discovery and readiness phase, including:

- Site survey.
- Site readiness.
- Network readiness.
- Application readiness.
- Operations readiness.

It also includes the following deliverables from the design phase:

System Design

- Existing system design diagram.
- New system design diagram.
- System design description document.

Feature and Function Design (optional, depending on the solution)

- Feature and function design description document.
- Feature and function summary listing for each major component.

Physical Design

- Existing physical design diagram.
- New physical design diagram.
- Physical design description document.

Device-level Design

- Device-level design description document.
- Device-level summary listing for each major component.

Operations Design

- Operations design description document.

Project Management Plan

The overall project management plan that was created during the design phase of the Services Lifecycle is the most important document for this implementation phase. It contains all the key data and information you need to manage and complete the implementation.

It is assumed that you have professional Project Managers in your implementation and technical delivery teams, and that these managers are certified as PMO professionals who are skilled with project management principles, methodologies, approaches, and guidelines.

One of these Project Management professionals should be assigned to each Implementation project and will be responsible for creating and managing the overall Implementation Project Plan (Master Project Plan).

> **TIP:** *Project Management tools and platforms have come a long way over the past decade and are now incredibly valuable to project and program managers, and to any organization, as they include online collaboration and work management features note previously available.*
>
> *One of these platforms to consider for any project or program management engagement is Smartsheet (www.smartsheet.com).*
>
> *This application includes many pre-defined templates that can very easily be applied to typical IT solution planning and implementation projects. Another advantage of a platform like Smartsheet is that all sheets, reports, and dashboards are online, and updates can be made collaboratively in real-time across all teams. This creates a single source of truth.*

You should treat the master project management plan you created for this implementation as a living document. The project manager should update it on a regular basis as resource allocations change and as other situations arise that require modifications to the plan. The master project plan also should serve as the primary mechanism for reporting progress to project sponsors.

Escalation Plan

In addition to the master project plan, another important document is the escalation plan. This plan describes the actions, processes, and procedures to escalate and resolve any issues that may arise during the implementation that could adversely affect the outcome of the engagement or the delivery date. These issues, in turn, may drive changes to the master project plan.

Communications Plan

The communications plan, another key document from the design phase, describes:

- The types of communications that need to occur between the implementation team and other customer teams.
- Communications with customer management and executive staff.
- All reporting requirements.
- The format and frequency of all communications.
- Key reporting dates and key meeting or review dates. Be sure to include these dates in the master project plan so that you can manage them appropriately.

Project Kick-Off Meetings

Prior to the start of any implementation project, schedule an internal project kick-off meeting with all key internal stakeholders. In this meeting, discuss all aspects of the implementation and identify any potential risks and issues.

At the end of this internal meeting, the project manager should have a clear understanding of what needs to be accomplished and should create an action plan to handle any potential issues that have been discussed.

> **TIP:** *As organizations and teams become more geographically dispersed, and as technology advances, it is becoming more and more typical and possible to run complex projects while collaborating with various team members remotely, using web conferencing and team collaboration technologies, such as Zoom, Cisco Webex, Microsoft Skype for Business, Slack, etc.*
>
> *It is highly recommended to invest in one or more of these collaboration tools.*

After the internal project kick-off meeting, the project manager and account manager should schedule the customer-facing project kick-off meeting. All key customer stakeholders should be invited to this meeting. The agenda should include an overview of all aspects of the implementation, a discussion of any potential issues, and an explanation of how they will be handled.

Key Steps for Project Planning

The key steps for this part of the process for all engagements are as follows:

- Verify and organize all content from previous phases.
    - Perform a gap analysis to verify that all implementation content is available.
    - Collect any missing or incomplete content based on the gap analysis.
    - Ascertain that the design documents all aspects of the solution.
    - Make sure that all planning documents have the detail required.
- Be sure that the following documents are complete and available:
    - Project management Plan.
    - Escalation Plan.
    - Communications Plan.
- Verify that the customer has approved the detailed design and the schedule.
- Make all content available to the implementation team.
- Schedule the internal and customer-facing project kick-off meetings.

Action Plan

Follow these action plan steps to implement this component of the guide in your organization:

Step	Action
Step 1.	Create a checklist for gathering solution design and deployment content.
Step 2.	Assign ownership of collecting this content to the implementation lead
Step 3.	Ensure that all engagement content is submitted to the knowledge management system.
Step 4.	Setup a communications tool to share content across the implementation team.

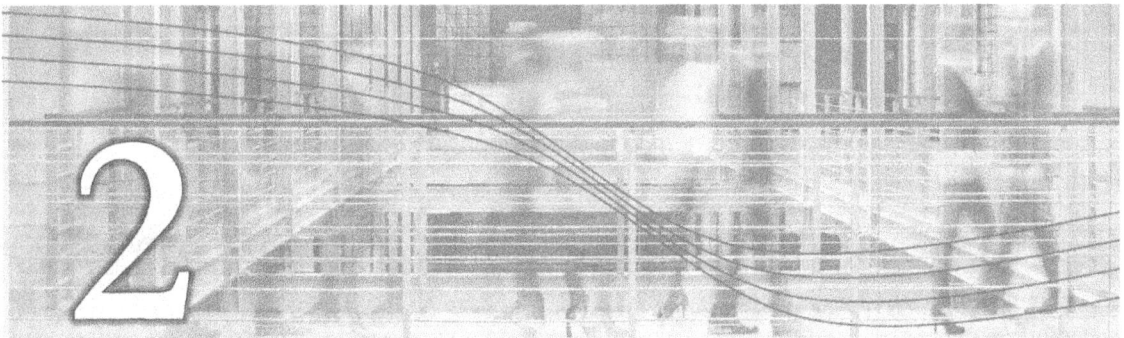

Chapter 2. Solution Staging

Staging is the process by which the hardware and software are prepared and tested, and the core systems are installed for the project deployment.

Staging may include physically preparing the equipment, loading the software, and reviewing the planning activities and other logistics prior to installing the core system. In addition, staging provides the following benefits.

- Ensures availability of all required networking, hardware, software and other project equipment.
- Centralizes location of key project materials.
- Provides opportunity to revisit implementation plan and work out shipping, receiving and delivery logistics for physical components.
- Confirms that core systems are functioning properly.
- Confirms that all systems are available for primary project activities prior to implementation.

Once the equipment has been identified, cataloged and prepared, core equipment can be installed in preparation for the primary project, which was defined in the staging and implementation plan during the design phase.

Key Steps for Staging

The key steps for this part of the process for all engagements are as follows:

- Assemble, inventory and organize hardware, software and any other project equipment.
- Install core system components identified in the staging plan.
- Configure platforms, devices, and applications as documented in the staging plan.

- Execute test cases as documented in the staging plan.

Action Plan

Follow these action plan steps to implement this component of the guide in your organization:

Step	Action
Step 1.	Create checklists for staging activities
Step 2.	Create sample staging plan templates.
Step 3.	Create sample equipment list templates.
Step 4.	Create standard processes and procedures for logistics management, including equipment ordering, packaging, shipping, and delivery.
Step 5.	Create sample hardware implementation project plans.
Step 6.	Create sample hardware implementation checklists for all major hardware components used in a typical solution.
Step 7.	Establish a logistics group within your organization to handle all procurement, delivery, and shipping activities associated with customer engagements.
Step 8.	Establish policies and procedures to handle equipment failure and replacement on installation.

Chapter 3. Phased implementation

It may be possible to deploy a new system or solution in one complete operation. However, in most cases, a complex system requires various parts of the solution to be implemented in phases over time. Therefore, one of the key deliverables from the design framework is the phased implementation plan. The phased implementation plan describes all the various phases that comprise the full solution, along with the specific steps to be completed in each phase. The phased implementation plan also addresses items that have cross-phase dependencies.

As shown below, the overall process may have phases that must occur sequentially, phases that can start simultaneously, phases that run in parallel, phases that have different time spans, and phases that are dependent on other phases. However, all phases must be complete before the solution is fully deployed.

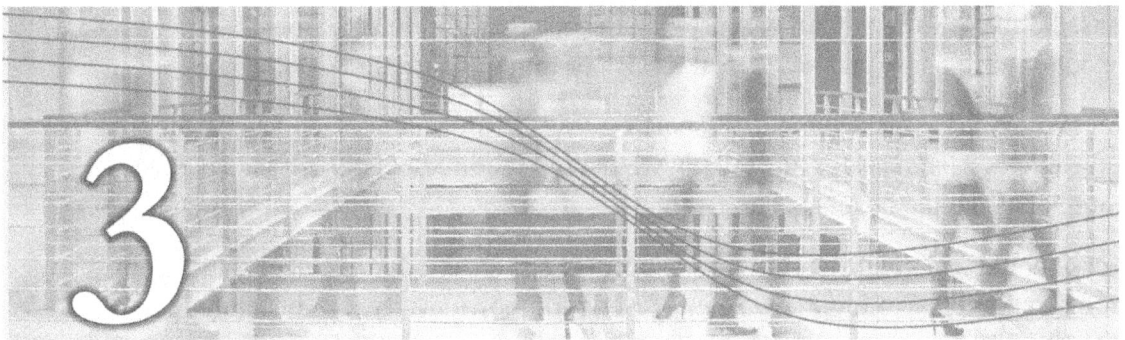

Figure 2. Sample Phased Implementation Diagram (Smartsheet Template Example)

The phased implementation plan will provide the detailed steps and actions to be completed for each phase and any dependencies or timing restrictions.

From an overall phase management perspective, you should also include a verification step at the end of each phase. This will ensure that all required actions for a step have been completed and the next step can begin.

Each phase could include different types of activities such as actual device installation, hardware installation, cabling, networking, configuration, and software installation. A phase also could consist of other activities such as scheduling and delivering user training sessions, or logistics activities such as ordering parts and components.

Because of these diverse requirements, make sure to schedule and allocate your technical deployment resources accordingly.

Solution Implementation

The first phase of the implementation project covers the physical installation of the hardware components comprising the solution. It relies upon the physical design documents and the feature and function design documents from the design framework.

Hardware implementation involves physically installing all hardware components. Therefore, you must first make sure that all required hardware is either available or on order through the appropriate procurement channels.

The customer may need to create or issue various purchase orders, or your organization may need to order the equipment. For larger engagements, you should assign a logistics manager to manage the ordering, scheduling, tracking, stocking, delivery, and allocation of all hardware components required for the implementation.

Further, deployments for larger engagements often span multiple locations. In these cases, make sure to deliver the required hardware to the target locations prior to the installation date. Also consider making additional items available in case of hardware failures.

In addition to "intelligent" hardware devices, such as servers, routers, switches, and communications devices, the implementation will include installing any required cables, power, and equipment racks. You should schedule the latter items for installation prior to the intelligent devices.

In some cases, the implementation team will need to coordinate with network service providers or external networking and communications providers for external connectivity requirements. The project manager should manage and schedule these communications services and include them in the master implementation project plan.

The hardware implementation phase also includes building, construction, and preparation — specifically, any security-related preparation. Of course, the actual building and construction is not part of the solution implementation. If required to support the new installation, or for added security, however, these activities must be completed before any hardware implementation can begin. Therefore, be sure to account for this type of ancillary activity in the implementation schedule.

Pilot Implementation and Testing

For most engagements, a pilot system migration, or pilot implementation, precedes the system migration phase. The purpose of the pilot implementation is to test the solution design and the implementation procedures and processes before moving on to the full implementation phase. The test is usually conducted for a small group of users, or a small division of the company.

To ensure comprehensive testing, the pilot implementation usually includes as many aspects of the full implementation as possible. For this reason, you should include all the standard installation, configuration, migration, and testing processes and procedures defined for the full implementation.

Similarly, the pilot implementation activities you include should mirror the standard activities defined in the master project implementation plan for the full implementation. As a result, all these aspects will be tested before system migration.

During the pilot phase, be certain to document and resolve all issues, and make appropriate changes to the master project implementation plan, so that you can avoid those issues during the full implementation.

Once you have completed the pilot implementation, fully test it to ensure that the system design meets the original specifications for the solution.

If you encounter any problems during these tests, escalate them to the design team and resolve them before moving on to the full implementation phase.

Device Implementation

Once all the basic hardware components have been installed, including equipment racks, power, and cabling, and the pilot test has been completed, you can begin deployment of the solution devices.

Prior to starting this phase, you should:

- Obtain the detailed specifications, the detailed connectivity requirements, and the configuration requirements for all the individual devices.
- Be sure that the installation schedule includes the staging, sequencing, and delivery of devices to be installed in various locations.
- Verify that the team has the required knowledge to properly configure and install the devices, which may require additional resource scheduling and allocation. Some devices may require a combination of hardware and software configurations.

Using the system design and the feature and function design documents, you can install and configure the various devices included in the solution. Next, you can connect the cabling and integrate the devices into the existing infrastructure. The project manager should coordinate this step to minimize the impact on the users and the existing systems.

You may want to deploy systems by group or building, or you may want to use a controlled rollout that allows both systems to run in parallel until the new systems are fully in place.

Note that most device manufacturers manufacture different models of the same device. In many cases, these models also may have different firmware versions and configuration and functionality options. Be sure to take all aspects into consideration so that you order and deliver the correct device types, models, and firmware levels for installation.

In all cases, consult the vendor's web site and technical documentation for detailed device specifications relating to the equipment being implemented.

Key Steps for Phased Implementation

The key steps for this part of the process for all engagements are as follows:

- Verify equipment received against the BOM (Bill of Materials).
- Assign ownership of individual phases to suitable technical leads.
- Assign ownership of equipment distribution and delivery to the logistics lead.
- Assign and make available suitable deployment resources for each phase.
- Prepare the customer environment for the implementation.
- Install, configure, integrate, and test the infrastructure, the clients, and related services.

- Test implementation activities during the pilot phase of the project.
- Manage the deployment of each phase, so that any interdependencies are adhered to and each phase is completed in sequence and to specification.
- Document the implemented components, devices, and applications.
- Host a hand-off and support introduction meeting.

Action Plan

Follow these action plan steps to implement this component of the guide in your organization:

Step	Action
Step 1.	Create checklists for implementation activities.
Step 2.	Create sample implementation project plan templates.
Step 3.	Create sample equipment list templates.
Step 4.	Create standard processes and procedures for logistics management, including equipment ordering, packaging, shipping, and delivery.
Step 5.	Create sample hardware implementation project plans.
Step 6.	Create sample hardware implementation checklists for all major hardware components used in a typical solution.
Step 7.	Develop and publish standard policies and procedures for subcontractors.
Step 8.	Create and publish sample equipment lists for typical engagements.
Step 9.	Establish a logistics group within your organization to handle all procurement, delivery, and shipping activities associated with customer engagements.
Step 10.	Establish policies and procedures to handle equipment failure and replacement on installation.

Chapter 4. Full System Migration

The full system migration moves the customer from one platform to a completely new environment without a staggered or phased timeline. This type of migration might also be called a "cutover" migration. It includes activities such as network migration, security migration, application migration, data migration, and device and configuration migration. The overall objective is to make sure all existing functionality that should remain in place has been migrated over to the new solution and is fully operational.

A pilot phase would also be a prerequisite in the full system migration process. This will ensure a smooth transition from one system to another.

Full System Migration Process

Once you have successfully completed the pilot implementation, the full system migration can commence.

Before you start the migration, back up all existing systems and capture all existing configuration details. Then, if regression becomes necessary, you can restore all previous settings to their original condition.

In some system migrations, a newer device with greater functionality or additional features will replace an existing device. In this case, you must switch from the existing device to the new device while keeping all previously available features and functions operating as required.

In terms of applications and data, you will need to test all existing applications to be migrated to be sure they are compatible with the new system. If you find the applications to be incompatible, you must acquire a newer compatible version of the application or modify the application, so it will run on the new system. In some cases, the application may no longer be required or will be replaced by a newer one. In these situations, all previous functionality must be available in the new application.

In addition, you must migrate all required data associated with the existing application so that the data will be accessible to the new applications.

If the solution calls for a complete replacement of the existing system with the new system, all networking equipment, applications, data, and device components must be installed and tested prior to switching from the old system to the new solution.

Then finally, the new solution must be at least as secure as the previous solution but is typically more secure than the previous solution. After the migration, make sure that all security aspects for the solution are operational and fully tested.

Key Steps for System Migration

In general, the key steps for this part of the process for all engagements are as follows:

- Prepare for full system migration.
- Track and verify dependency milestones.
- Execute the full migration plan.
- Identify all systems to be migrated from the system design and migration planning documentation.
- Identify all application compatibility issues and create a mitigation plan for each.
- Remedy all applications that have been identified as being incompatible.
- Identify all data transformation requirements; test and document all transformation procedures.
- Determine any staging and location details for system migration.
- Create a list of all the system components that will need to be migrated, including hardware, devices, applications, and data.
- Install and test all target system components.
- Create a migration back-out and regression plan.
- Ensure that the existing systems are fully backed up prior to migration.
- If possible, test all migration tasks prior to the actual migration.
- Create detailed migration and configuration sheets for each system component to be migrated.

- Include all detailed system migration tasks into the master implementation project plan.
- Schedule the appropriate technical resources for system migration and configuration.
- Test all systems that have been migrated to ensure all functionality and features are available.
- Host a hand-off meeting for the customer operations team.

Action Plan

Follow these action plan steps to implement this component of the guide in your organization:

Step	Action
Step 1.	Create sample system migration project plans.
Step 2.	Create sample system migration checklists for all major devices used in a typical solution.
Step 3.	Develop and publish standard policies and procedures for system migration.
Step 4.	Create and publish sample system backup-and-restore procedures and checklists.
Step 5.	Create and publish sample system migration test plans.

Chapter 5. Acceptance Testing

Once you have deployed the solution and have identified and resolved all initial issues, the next step entails conducting a series of acceptance tests on the new solution.

The parameters for the system acceptance-testing phase were previously defined in the design phase and agreed to by the customer. The implementation team should have access to this information to validate the functionality of the new solution.

During acceptance testing, the team should test every aspect of the new solution for conformance with the original solution requirements. A suitable customer representative must be present during these acceptance tests to approve every successful test.

You should plan to conduct the system acceptance testing in an iterative manner. This means that on the first pass, you would test all system components and note any out-of-line situations. You then address and remedy any outstanding issues or inoperable functions. Continue with a second pass of all the tests and repeat the process until the customer has approved every system component.

During this phase, be sure to have the original engagement scope details on hand. It is quite possible that the customer will request functions or features that were not originally included in the solution design and scope. If this occurs, bring the out-of-scope request to the customer's attention. The customer should open a change request if the function or feature is indeed required.

Key Steps for Acceptance Testing

The key steps for this part of the process for all engagements are as follows:

- Using the acceptance test plan developed during the design phase, identify all tests that need to be completed.

- Create acceptance test checklists for each test to be run. These checklists should contain an area for the customer to approve.

- Schedule a suitable time to conduct the tests when the customer representative is present.

- Run all system acceptance tests and sign off those tests that complete successfully.

- Capture all details relating to any test that does not complete successfully.

- If one or more tests have failed, identify the cause and remedy the situation.

- If any changes are made to the system design, setup, or configuration, ensure that these changes are reflected in the system documentation.

- Once all remediation is complete, reschedule the acceptance tests.

- If substantial changes have been made to the system, re-run all system acceptance tests.

- Run the system acceptance tests again, with the customer representative present, and have the customer approve all tests that successfully complete.

- Repeat the above steps, if necessary, to ensure that all system tests run successfully.

- Report back to the customer sponsor and to your account team on the successful completion of the system acceptance tests.

Action Plan

Follow these action plan steps to implement this component of the guide in your organization:

Step	Action
Step 1.	Create sample system acceptance testing project plans.
Step 2.	Create sample system acceptance testing checklists for all major components used in a typical solution.
Step 3.	Develop and publish standard policies and procedures for system acceptance testing.
Step 4.	Create and publish sample system acceptance testing reports and templates.

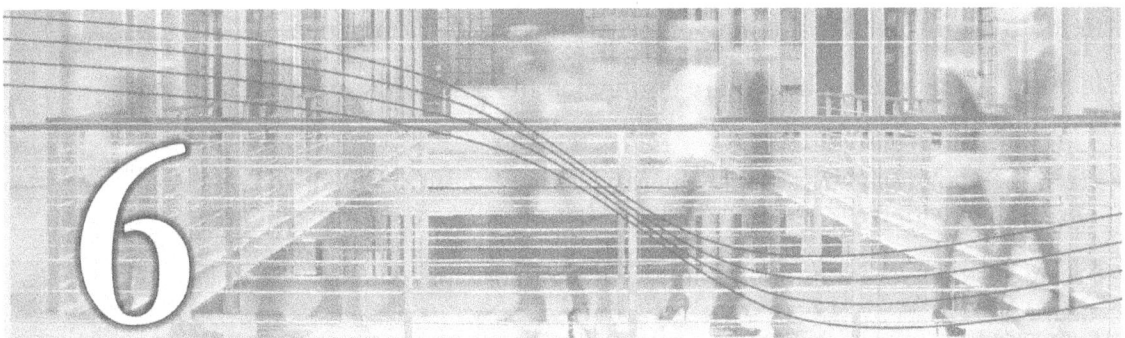

Chapter 6. Staff Training
End User Training

In most cases, when deploying a new solution for a customer, the system will introduce new functionality and new features and may operate differently from the existing system. Therefore, end users will require training to use the new solution. The content and details of the end user training should surface during the design phase of the engagement. This training content should be made available to the trainers and should be incorporated into the schedule as part of the implementation phase.

The training may be as simple as showing end users how to use a new advanced telephony system when they previously used a simple telephone system. On the other hand, if they switched to a more complex communications solution, the training would involve more complex tasks, such as accessing their messages through a new user interface, or through voice commands.

In either case, strive to train the end users on the new solution at the right time. Providing end-user training too early may increase help desk calls, since the users may have forgotten aspects of the training. Providing the end user training too late may result in users not being able to do their jobs properly.

Include the end user training schedules in the master implementation project plan so that users receive the required training at the right time and in the most appropriate location.

The customer help desk staff also should receive the training and have access to the content to help them to better understand and resolve end user issues after the solution has been fully deployed.

Key Steps for End User Training

The key steps for this part of the process for all engagements are as follows:

- Refer to the formal staff training plan generated in the design phase.
- Identify all end users who require training on the new solution, including their roles and locations.
- From the implementation plans, determine what training content should be delivered to which users, and the most suitable time to deliver that content.
- Create an end user training schedule, with content type, dates, times, and locations.
- Work with the customer to schedule end user training courses and ensure that suitable training facilities and logistics are arranged.
- Schedule suitably trained trainers to deliver the end user training in the assigned locations.
- Provide all the required training content to the trainers, as well as any required course material.
- Include all end user training activities in the master implementation project plan.

Action Plan

Follow these action plan steps to implement this component of the guide in your organization:

Step	Action
Step 1.	Determine whether your organization will provide end user training services or will use subcontractors.
Step 2.	If your organization will provide this training, establish a training group.
Step 3.	If using subcontractors, establish suitable relationships, including subcontractor agreements and standard rate cards.
Step 4.	Create a library of training content of all common end user training requirements.
Step 5.	Publish all available end user training offerings to the knowledge management system.
Step 6.	Publish all available end user training content to the knowledge management system.
Step 7.	If your organization is providing this service, verify that your trainers are capable and certified as required.

Administrator and Help Desk Training

If administrative and help desk training services were included in the operational support plan and the statement of work, you can provide training to the customer administrative and help desk staff on all aspects of the solution, including:

- The system design, the devices and applications deployed, and all aspects of system operation.
- The processes and procedures for monitoring and managing the system.
- How to keep all functions and features of the solution operating according to plan.
- The processes and procedures for handling and resolving all end user issues.

As described in the design framework, this training can either be delivered by your organization or by a third party certified training organization. In either case, however, you should customize the training content to the specifics of the customer solution as deployed.

You might need to repeat the training classes several times, since not all the customer administrative and help desk staff may be able to attend training classes at the same time. Record these sessions, if possible, to provide content for refresher training and to train new staff.

In either facilitated or lecturer-led training classes, the training should include documentation about the system, specifically guides and handbooks describing the operational procedures for the solution.

Provide information about additional technical training resources and courses to the customer staff during this phase of the engagement. Include a recommendation for additional ongoing training that the staff should consider.

Key Steps for Administrator and Help Desk Training

The key steps for this part of the process for all engagements are as follows:

- Refer to the formal staff training plan generated in the design phase.
- Identify all administrative and help desk staff members who require training on the new solution, including their roles and locations.
- From the implementation plans, determine what training content will need to be delivered to which staff, and the most suitable time to deliver that content.

- Create an administrative and help desk training schedule, with content type, dates, times, and locations.
- Work with the administrative and help desk staff to schedule training courses and ensure that suitable training facilities and logistics are arranged.
- Schedule suitably trained instructors to deliver the training in the assigned locations.
- Provide all the required training content and any required course material to the instructors.
- Include all training activities in the master project implementation plan.

Action Plan

Follow these action plan steps to implement this component of the guide in your organization:

Step	Action
Step 1.	Determine whether your organization will provide administrative and help desk training services or will use subcontractors.
Step 2.	If your organization will provide this training, establish a training group.
Step 3.	If using subcontractors, establish suitable relationships, including subcontractor agreements and standard rate cards.
Step 4.	Create a library of training content of all common administrative and help desk training requirements.
Step 5.	Publish all available administrative and help desk training offerings to the knowledge management system.
Step 6.	Publish all available administrative and help desk training content to the knowledge management system.
Step 7.	If your organization is providing this service, verify that your trainers are capable and certified as required.

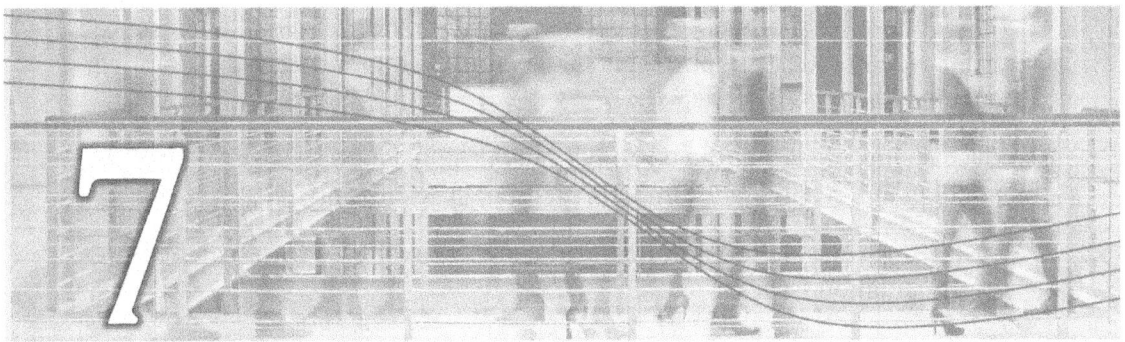

Chapter 7. Post Implementation Support

After fully implementing the solution, your technical staff should be available to the end users and the customer's technical support staff to quickly resolve any implementation issues. Plan to provide this support coverage for at least the first day after the implementation has been completed (Day One Support).

It may be possible to use the customer help desk facility for Day One implementation support, which will have the added benefit of providing exposure and knowledge transfer for the customer help desk staff.

For Day One after full implementation, your technical implementation team, as well as your technical architect team, should quickly identify and resolve any issues. Provide multiple methods for opening support issues, including telephone call-in, on-site technical staff, and email or portal options.

Also schedule escalation support options for Day One support. That way, the staff can escalate any manufacturer-related issues to the manufacturer for resolution.

Key Steps for Post Implementation Support

The key steps for this part of the process for all engagements are as follows:

- Place the implementation team on-site to provide coverage and support for Day One post implementation. Be sure to identify and resolve any implementation issues rapidly and completely.
- Day One – Handoff Meeting:
    - Provide suitably trained technical staff at each remote location for post implementation.

- o Provide a call-in number to all end users and provide an email address for end users to request support (this may be the customer's help desk number and email address).
- o Place technical staff at the customer help desk location to assist with handling and resolving all implementation issues that arise.
- o Ensure that the solution architect and team are available for escalation of implementation issues.
- o Create a support contract and procedures to escalate manufacturer-related issues to the manufacturers, if necessary.
- o Provide procedures and processes to the customer support staff to communicate to all end users about how to open a support incident.
- o Make sure that customer support staff can differentiate between an implementation issue and a regular help desk issue. Regular help desk issues should be handled in the normal way, through standard help desk procedures.
- If any remedial action occurs that involves a change to the implemented system, capture the changes and record them in the solution documentation.

Action Plan

Follow these action plan steps to implement this component of the guide in your organization:

Step	Action
Step 1.	Establish an in-house support help desk that can also be used for post-implementation support, when this offering is specified in the statement of work.
Step 2.	Ensure that your organization has support agreements in place with all vendors and major manufacturers so that you can escalate implementation issues, if necessary.
Step 3.	Capture all implementation issues and resolutions in the knowledge management system.

Chapter 8. Operations Implementation

Once the solution is fully deployed and all tests have been completed and approved by the customer, you can begin deploying the operations plan. This phase will include the implementation of certain monitoring and management systems, but most of the activities will relate to the policies, processes, and procedures. As a result, any issues that arise can be detected and resolved quickly.

These policies, processes, and procedures enable the operations staff to effectively monitor and manage the solution. They should cover how to use the system, capacity planning, performance monitoring, system maintenance, backups, disaster recovery, and reporting.

The operations implementation derives all its detail from the operations plan and operations design documents. At a high level, the operations implementation should cover:

- System monitoring.
- Incident management.
- Problem management.
- Change management.
- Configuration management.
- Supplier management.
- Security administration.

These activities will be explained in detail in the implementation plan.

Key Steps for Operations Implementation

The key steps for this part of the process for all engagements are as follows:

- Identify all operations components, policies, and procedures to be deployed from the operations design and operations plan documentation.
- Determine any staging and location details for operations implementation.
- Include all operations implementation activities in the master project plan.
- Ensure that suitable technical staff members can install all operations systems.
- Create a list of all the devices required, including model numbers, types, firmware levels, and any other associated components, such as required software.
- Schedule any operations hardware and software components to be installed.
- Ensure that all required applications and management systems are installed.
- Create all detailed policies, processes, and procedures required.
- Procure all necessary product manuals from the manufacturers, as required.
- Configure all systems monitoring and management devices and applications.
- Test all operations systems, applications and management devices.

Action Plan

Follow these action plan steps to implement this component of the guide in your organization:

Step	Action
Step 1.	Create sample operations implementation project plans.
Step 2.	Create sample operations implementation checklists for all major operations systems and procedures used in a typical solution.
Step 3.	Develop and publish standard policies and procedures for operations implementation, including standard templates.
Step 4.	Ensure that all operations implementation documentation from customer engagements is captured in the knowledge management system.
Step 5.	Create a library of information relating to all operations support systems and applications from other vendors and publish it to the knowledge management system.

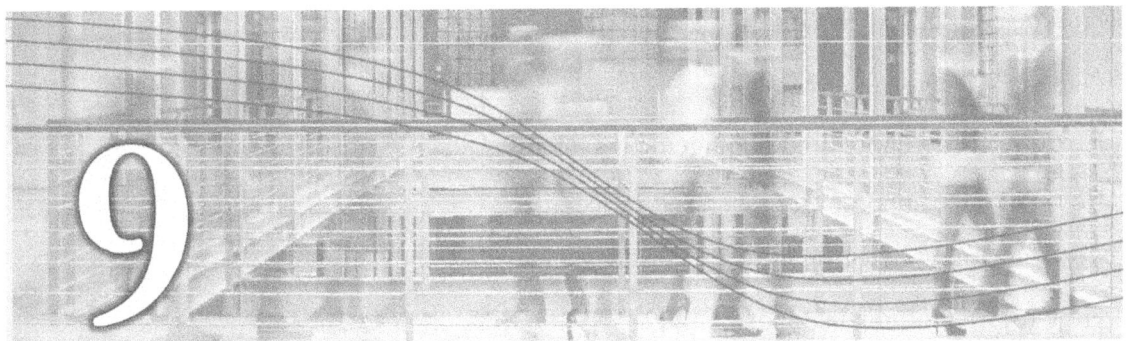

Chapter 9. Project Closeout

The project closeout meeting should be scheduled after the solution has been fully deployed. Invite the key customer support and help desk leads to this meeting. Facilitators for the meeting itself should include the implementation lead, the project manager, and the account manager from your organization. Also include the technical architects from both organizations.

After fully installing, configuring, and testing the solution, update the original documentation and plans, and then collate all content to form the *as-built documentation*.

The as-built documentation consists of all the content and documentation that adequately describes the complete solution as it has been implemented. The customer technical staff receives it when the project is complete, and it serves as a reference going forward.

The as-built documentation becomes training reference material when the customer administrative and help desk staff receive training on the solution. It provides ongoing support for the maintenance of the solution.

The as-built documentation should be compiled and presented to the customer when the solution is handed over. This as-built documentation package can be in the form of printed documents, but most typically it will be in an electronic form, and made available through an online portal, or a set of files.

A good option here is to make the documentation available on an access restricted customer specific portal that your company owns. This provides a common reference, and a way to ensure that the customer will come back to your portal regularly. This is another possible way of differentiating your organization from your competition.

The agenda for the project closeout meeting may include the following items:

- Overview of the complete solution.

- Overview of the solution design.
- Overview of the implementation.
- Review of the support and management systems.
- Review of the support processes and procedures.
- Review of the escalation procedures.
- How to get additional support.
- Additions and extensions to the solution.
- Review of all solution and support documentation.
- Final hand-over.

It should be made clear to the customer staff during this meeting that the handover has been completed and that the responsibility of the solution now rests with the customer support team.

Key Steps for Project Closeout

The key steps for this part of the process for all engagements are as follows:

- Arrange an internal preparation meeting with the solution architect and the implementation team to review all aspects of the solution implementation.
- Identify all outstanding issues and resolve them.
- Have the solution architect and the implementation lead create a set of presentations to be used during the meeting.
- Schedule the meeting and invite all key customer staff and the key staff from your organization.
- Have the solution architect and the implementation lead present the details of the implementation.
- Present all final solution documentation to the customer.
- Make the customer aware of any additional services that your organization can provide to further enhance the solution.

Action Plan

Follow these action plan steps to implement this component of the guide in your organization:

Step	Action
Step 1.	Create and publish a standard checklist for the project closeout meeting.
Step 2.	Create and publish sample meeting agendas for the project closeout meeting.
Step 3.	Create presentation templates and sample presentations for the project closeout meeting.
Step 4.	Ensure that all relevant technical staff members are trained on presentation techniques.
Step 5.	Establish a standard documentation-packaging format that represents your organization.
Step 6.	Publish all information, templates, and checklists to the knowledge management system.

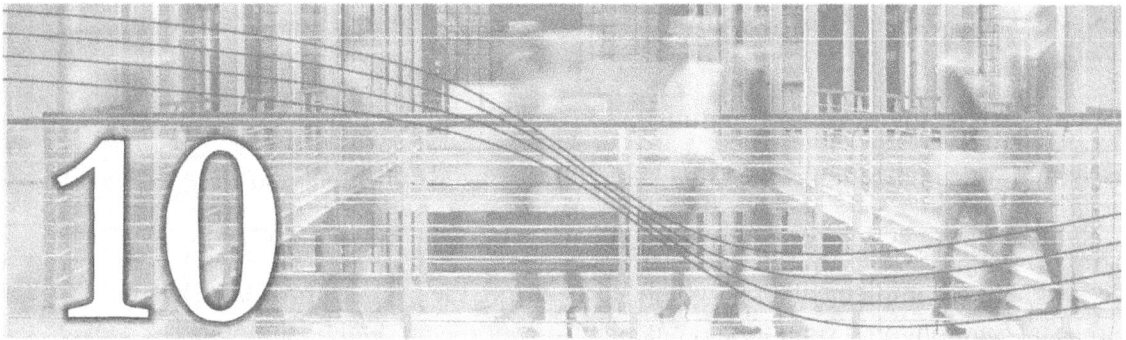

Chapter 10: How to Measure Your Success

To gauge the success of your business, you should analyze and measure the effectiveness of the activities associated with each practice component. Setting proper goals, evaluating staff performance, and measuring the positive or negative results of your business actions will help build success. Likewise, measuring and evaluating the results after applying the concepts and practices suggested in this document will help determine the success of your business.

As a benchmark for successful implementations, you should measure and ensure that:

- All systems are fully operational.
- The solution is aligned with the original business plan.
- All outages are identified and resolved within acceptable limits and any changes are implemented smoothly.
- Operations staff and users are fully trained.
- Responsibilities are transferred to the operations group.

From a business perspective, you should develop metrics to evaluate the overall effectiveness of your implementation framework. Some of the areas to consider are:

- Services delivery ready content for implementation framework is available.
- Formalized customer acceptance criteria plan identifies tests to be conducted and what documented results will serve as success criteria.
- Implementation guidelines are defined for staging, hardware implementation, legacy integration, device deployment, system migration, and operation implementation.

- System acceptance testing is outlined for various stages of the implementation process.
- End-user training as well as administration and helpdesk training are established.
- As-built documentation is included as part of the hand-off.
- Number of projects successfully implemented on time and within budget.

A successful solution implementation, which starts during the presales process, ends by setting the stage for ongoing support and customer development. Establishing and executing the best practices in this document along with evaluating their effectiveness will give you a platform for growth, increased business profitability, and overall success.

www.ingramcontent.com/pod-product-compliance
Lightning Source LLC
Chambersburg PA
CBHW081020170526
45158CB00010B/3114